THERE IS NO FALLING

Robert Hogg

Copyright © Robert Hogg, 1993.
All rights reserved.

Canadian Cataloguing in Publication Data

Hogg, Robert, 1942-
    There is no falling

Poems.
ISBN 1-55022-198-1

I. Title
PS8565.O55T54 1993   C811'.54   C93-094249-3
PR9199.3.H75T54 1993

The general editor of ECW poetry books is Bruce Whiteman.

Cover photo by Leslie Hogg. Photo of the author by Cyrus Hogg.

Published with the assistance of The Canada Council
and the Ontario Arts Council.

Designed and set in Cartier by ECW Type & Art, Oakville, Ontario.

Distributed by General Distribution Services,
30 Lesmill Road, Toronto, Ontario M3B 2T6.

Published by ECW Press,
1980 Queen Street East, Toronto, Ontario M4L 1J2.

There Is No Falling

For Ted Zuber
who provided the Vivaldi
& a perfect day
for sketching poems
all the best
   Bob Hilles
    '94

for Ethan, Cyrus and Sarada

So Much for Enclosures

Better to live in the open
I always say

If you don't look back
there's never any

tracks in the still
falling snow

And walking ahead
when the air's

this crisp
you can see the shape

of silence
every breath

Extreme Positions *(for bp*

    The lovely play language is .   The lay of the poem .

      The place maide .   The dropping or adding of a letter .

        Tension .   Love crosses all bodies

          of water   or of land

              vi
              o
              le
              (n)
              t

Love knows its own bounds
    but crosses these
        willingly
knows to stay
stray
    brings the point of light
right up to the eye

knows that all event
is also a screen
    retina
      page
where the hand trembles
to leave a mark in

              v
              i
              o
              l
              a
              t
              e

                space

so great the mind's
demand
that a map be drawn
lines be drawn
against chaos
but also
break the edge

Put an S on things.   Put S in the world.   Sing

                silent
                 p
                 a
                 c
                spell
                o   i
                u   g
                n   h
              words standing
                 a
                 l
                 o
                 n
                essential

free .   The lovely play   love is   a language made

                sign

(against unknowing

Midnight

Midnight and that
being later than
I want it to be

and me thinking
or not able
not to think

there being that
distinction
how strangely

the world
or at least that
part of it

we come to
inhabit
simply falls

asleep goes
out shuts
the door

good
night

Postmodern Perplex

The body as a place
to spend time in

imperfect vehicle
complete with pain

You can take it
(me) almost

anywhere
you care to

and if you don't
that's alright

too — I've been
known to wait

    2 *(for* M C *Escher*

Whatever else you
do don't
let one
hand know
what the other

    3

Looking back on
a life/sentence
without
period. Who
do you think
you are?

4

Crazy this music
that follows the
body around
close, close
to the chest
as though all
along it knew
the correct
steps to
the dance

5

This tissue
by which we hold
to what we call
life

    What's all the issue
about a lil' tissue

said
twenty years away
if a day

where is that
thought now
that I bring
it here

both places
in time?
a similar
bar

    music playing
its own
background
to a general

noise of voices
people come here
to eat

    Don't
give them this
by mistake

    6

How then not
miss
take what
others leave

We come on
this past
presently
prey

on old
propositions
memories
ago

Don't think
I don't
think of
you

there when
you
come
here

A Purple Flower (for my daughter

This poppy
you want me
to buy

and can't
understand
why

I don't
wear one
proudly

What can you
think of
me

in your innocent
desire
to wear a flower

   *

How shall I tell
you of the war
I was born into

of my father
who fought
four years

in the trenches
the war
before that

where poppies
grew like buttons
of blood undone

    *

If I drop these
coins in a card-
board box

if I wear this
plastic
flower

in my lapel
will I buy
peace

or does this
emblem
celebrate

war itself
the glory
of dying young

    *

In my mind the dead
go on crying
against the living

who parade old
victories
out to the cenotaphs

with ritual
piety each
Remembrance Day

On their navy
blue blazers
the bright

red poppies
cry out
for further blood

    *

So why not leave
the poppies in
Flanders fields

pick instead
some wild
outlandish flower

too gaudy and large
to fit in any
buttonhole

If we must
live a nightmare
let us dream

a wild insanity
of flowers
a kind of

Easter
out of season
a world

overgrown
with exotic
orchids

thick
as a fallen
snow

    *

Or let it rain
fuchsia and bleeding
hearts

until with one
accord
we yearn to climb

out of our anguish
out of our sing-
ular being

and bathe in the black
light the cool
brow soft

touch
leads us
wholly back

through Earth's
daughter Moon's
mother Hell's

keeper
until we regain
the dark

sun the negative
light we remember
making

a purple
seed
shaken

from the pod
and gently
eaten

or sown
on abundant
soil

    *

In our journey
to Eleusis
we have entered

Demeter's
temple
planted

in total
darkness
whatever seeds

we could garner
from Flanders
or imagined

fields
Persephone
long since

abducted
the mother
distraught

then angered
the sun
blacked out

    *

In absence
it happens

in the dark
it rises

amid much
crashing

of cymbals
and cries

of the votaries
the flower

blooms
Kora

appears
in perfect

nakedness
the Kouros

is born
a splendid

youth
fully formed

out of the dark-
ness out of

the blood
and fire

out of
the anguished

heart
a purple flower

Becoming Night (for Harry Flaig, artist

To tell the truth
when I look out my
west window I don't
see a snow-clad
log cabin
its neat row of windows
amber against
gathering dusk

What I see is
a blank pane of glass
and beyond that a man
reflected in the glass

(though I believe the building's
out there
what's left of it

it was never a log
cabin with smoke
curling from its chimney
never exactly
sequestered
a branching tree
in the foreground
as you chose
to paint it

but it's true
it does lean over
as the barren
hickory bends to
prevailing winds

What I come back to
this snowfallen
December night

is not a decrepit
shed about to
collapse

nor indeed the
predictable portent
beyond the glass

What haunts me
simply
is the picture

you imagined
standing inside
the window as I

do now imagining
in early evening
a skilled brush

catching the subtle
greys and muted
blues of winter

a yellow light
behind the windows
could be the sun

set caught in
the southwest
wall

it being that
time of day
becoming night

Robin Greenwood

Robin Greenwood
the man with
green sleeves
on fire

hides among
ashes and old
dead elms
hides

behind a log
stoking
the embers
into fire

There is soot
on his green
sleeve
soot

he carries with
him climbing
the stairs
from the furnace

up to the white
enamel
kitchen
sink

Flicks with his
finger soot
from green
sleeve

Sits down
quietly
with family
to watch TV

Balancing the World

I've never been
very good at
balancing the world

but these days
it all seems
piled up on me

as though there were
more weight in
the asking than

any burden carried
could rightly be
expected to

contain.   What
can I put down
and where lay

my head
so as not to
destroy the flow

nor unseat
the balanced
stone

Gaugin's Intimate Mangoes

Why if I do not
hate myself
have I stayed up
late drinking
beer and reading
your *Intimate*
Journals
while watching
the Saturday night
rock videos
ridiculous pop
life bursting
like these magnificent
mangoes confused
with Tahitian
Women
still life
spilling all
over the place
not me

Father Father

Father Father
when you died
it was not a
betrayal

I did not
blame you
for not
cutting off

your ear
(you were shav-
ing in the bath-
room do

you remember
the door
typically
locked

when you didn't
answer George
had to climb through
the window

to unlock
the door
why should I
blame you

for not
deserting
your family
years before

for not vanishing
to lost Tahitis
of the South
Pacific

your mind
neglected to
discover.
It was not

your fault
petty lust and not
grand desire
drove you on

or that nothing
like madness
leprosy
or syphilis

led you to
new heights
or that no
wounds bled

inextricably
during the long
night of
loneliness

marriage
and raising
children
had become

Mom and us
kids
squeezed
to the sidelines

that time E.D.
came up to
the Cariboo
from Edmonton

and we all went
picnicking
on the banks
of the North

Bonaparte
(E.D. travelling
to Clinton by bus
because she said

she just loved
bus drivers and you
drove in alone
in the '48 Dodge

one-ton to
pick her up)
and Sunday it
was hot we all

went to the
river not
to swim
the water

too cold
for that
and briskly
flowing

her long legs
a tangle
no summer skirt
could contain

and her shifting
this way and
that in the hot
mosquito sun

asking you to spread
was it repellant or
sun tan oil
on her calves

Mother trying
not to notice
George it might
have been down

river a bit
watching for
trout me
watching your hand

slide up smooth
calf and over
knee down
ankle me

watching the rhythm
of her breath
breasts in tight
fifties sweater

rising & falling
with the swell
Mother looking
everywhere else

for the sandwiches
and Kool Aid
and calling George
back for lunch

brushing mosquitoes
from her cotton
print dress ants
from the blanket

handing round
drinks home
made pickles
and bread

whatever hopeful
antidotes to
beauty and
desire

Early Morning, January

Though it's totally
    winterstruck and
        barren as death

the tree is the tree
    of life
        and the birds

(chickadee & gross-
    beak & several
        haughty jays

dust back &
    forth among the
        snowy

branches
    & the three
        swinging

bird feeders
    from which
        at each

swoop
    they deftly
        pick a

single
    sunflower
        seed

The Present (with thanks to Harry & Bea)

Let me come face
to face with the person
in my dream, whatever
rings true as this
Tibetan bell
moment beyond moment
rung with such
clarity it wakes both
heart and mind
locked in one
step the soul
hungering, hovering
a mystical wave   air
moving   rhythm
repeated
memory of monks
in trance
ringing
hour upon hour
worshippers up
the Mountain
Path
to the shrine

Why do we seek
what is already
held in mind / hand
rocking the *dorje*
hour on hour
     sound
an eternal presence
ringing through every
stone on Himalayan
hills

     And there is no
falling no falling
away
    from the pure
sound the clear
water
    running
downhill
       in the mountains

    I remember
the spring
at Arunachula
the old sanyassin
in their orange robes
removing their sandals
to bathe in
the holy pool
the stone so hot
you could hardly
look into it
the sun that intense
the water
equally cool

Falling Through Space

What struck me
dumb in Escher's
art

was sound
uplifting
silence

taut
      bent

words
strung at curious
angles of intent

the whole
structure
about to fall

into new
sentence
walls

inhere
to an old
harmonics

of the heart
a new
syntax

the hand's
light
touch

a string's
vibration
resonant

measure
of time
spent

falling through space

caught &
held
in the eye's

start
a visioned
world

held so
momently
lines

run in all
directions
make it still

A Possible Light

Here
I am
and it

is mid-
night
again

as though
a word
could stand

time
on its
head

dark a
rock
holds

everything
upside
down

*

What makes us
think
we will find

a way out of
obdurate
soil

send down
such roots
cunning

will teach us
how turn
the wheel

produces in
utter dark
a possible

light

Word (a Postmodern epic

Word walked into
the forest
of critical discontent

Was it love
or self-hate
made him seek out

the pool
of deepening
intent

lean over the edge
disturb the surface
with image reversed

*

Word looked at himself
(a mistake)
saw he was only

a four-letter word
all consonance
and avowal

a present
accumulation
constantly

sliding back
into something
said

*

Madly in love
Word slipped off
his consonants

dove
O-long
into the pool

Infinite rings
broke in promising
circles to the shore

*

Stript at last
of excess
verbiage

wOrd merged
with the deep
unknown

Immersed
in the great
ocean of bliss

he sang to himself
of the soul's
loneliness

O *solo me* O
he crooned
and contemplated

the great
nothingness
at the center of being

*

Thus, thought O
to himself,
(for so he had

become)
one reaches
the further shore

while still descending
within one's
essential being

Pleased with himself
O pursed his lips
to smile

air rings
rose from his mouth
wobbled toward

the surface
eager to be
born

then vanished
into the ether
from whence they came

O grew
silent
a Cartesian

diver
he calmly
drifted down

*

The sun went
down the moon
came up O

winced at the ob-
vious cliche
and remained submerged

Bones on the bottom
sent up pale
waves of light

(O caught their faded
splendor
within the luminous

circle
of his newly
created being

I'm a slipt
nimbus
a lost

oval
a suspended
and unsent

letter from
the Milky
Way

O moaned
while the moon
mimicked his form

Invisible tears
marred the absence of
cheeks

O faded
relentlessly
into the grey film of time

*

Perfectly merged
in the Great Pool
O became

Pure Thought
trying to recall
the words

he had previously
been   Nothing
occurred

O looked up
crying from
the void:

O Word
Why hast thou
forsaken me?

and the heavens
parted above
and the earth

was rent below
and a great roar
filled the abyss

*

Sore afraid
O clutched at his
midriff vowel

Gripped with despair
he strained
like a mighty

Titan against
denial
Nothing

since the Great
Flood or Pentecostal
Fire not even

the Grimm
Consonantal
Shift

or the gradual
loss of the
middle voice

had so undermined
the stability of
his power

*

Firmament
and fundament
clashed

Drop by drop
O's ur-thoughts
recongealed

With tremendous
effort
sounds gathered

weight and substance
matter
newly inhered

a world where there
had been nothing
gradually appeared

*

O found a green hill
and fell asleep
In a dark dream

he stood upon the mountain
of his invention
surveyed the world

he had made
and swelled once again
into tumescent Word

The great
nakedness of his
being empty

left him
(as a snake
sloughs his skin

beside a rock
and sometimes
a man

coming across
the spangle left
in the grass

picks it up
unwittingly
and seeing some

service in its shape
knots it about
his waist...

So Word
strode forth
once again

a magus
of meaning
a knight

in a burnished
allegory
of intent

already
a saint among
martyrs

bent on becoming
a sentence of
high repute

*

And Word gave up
the emptiness
and the desire

silence and
the deep well
of fear

He built in his image
a palace of
clear intent

The people
loved it and called
it the Perfect Meaning

Now pilgrims arrive
daily to worship
the Complete Sentence

consume the Divine
Paragraph whisper
the Final Word

A Kind of Nightlife

It was the night of my life
nothing as yet impossible
the dark already shining
like a moon in the wake of being

I could hear the sounds of my heart
singing against the far shore
I could hear the voice of my lover
sighing for love of me

Softly, softly I went to my love
it was like walking on water
like wading a tide-thick air
I hardly know what sustained me

If this is death, I thought,
I will go on loving forever.

A Disturbance of Words

It is already perfect why
would I want to
disturb it
with idiot words

love of language
or love of self
makes me look past
this oak-handled
hammer to the feel
of its wood the classic
knurl of its head so that
I pick it up   heft
it gently in my hand
and try my eyes on the faint
print I can just about
read because it is early
morning & my eyes have not
yet fallen to their daylong
lethargy

  outside
the newfallen snow
is heaven & Zep
our young black
dog runs
circles around the house

Roof

I took off part of a day of my life
and looked at it

words...
words...

I took off my glasses
rubbed my eyes

and looked again
at the read

page
written

blurred

Outside the window
the snow of a

neighbouring
roof

reached a perfect
exaltation

and began its
imperceptible

retreat

Amaryllis

I am sitting behind this amaryllis and it is no joke it is towering before me. It has four red heads & is not a giant but certainly it seems one. I say I am sitting behind it is so much in front of me I just feel that way so antiamaryllis so very unread. It seems to grow out of the round wicker table that centers the sun room & places me one side. It knows more about catching the sun in its red horn than I'll ever know. Even the pitcher of milk with its pink hearts & blue abstract flowers knows less of the sun than my right shoulder that warms. I write this in red ink in the heat of a March afternoon but I know it will not be read that way.

I come back again after a walk to sit with my mind in front of the four-headed amaryllis that is not a lamp shining on a book but a flower looking me in the face that might be

so strong on some occasions it confutes simple reality and calls for another description more abstruse and yet truer than a blue guitar which anyway I cannot play and can never be the man with

what concerns me again is the absorption & reflection of light and why when it hits the retina it leaves an indelible image

not the thing in itself or even the thought about the thing (in itself) but rather the passage of a flower from one state of being to another

Hard to believe it is actually upside down I mean not out there or finally in here this side of the computer but there where it first manifests itself as sight on the rod & cone

imagine what control it would take to turn off the processor & see from above down the floor & wicker table pot & long green stem

the four-headed trumpet blowing out at mid-eye-range space emptying out beneath it with half-focused open door to the sun room

blurred in the background a gist of tongue & groove ceiling panelling the bottom of the view and you gentle reader a smile reflected on your shoe

The other day it fell over I wasn't there and it fell over it just fell over that's all

when I first saw it tipped like that not just the stalk but pot and all I thought aha the cat did this the goddam cat and I knew which one of three

because this is the sun room where only Sprite hangs out and tries to shit & piss in the cactus and several times

she's got the worst of it but so have we well this time I was wrong I'm almost sure it just

fell over pot and all

Three Nude Sketches

Sketch 1

This stately pine
thrusts its yellow
buds against summer's
onset

what does it know
of the sun slants its
yellow light toward
the ground

the mating trill
robins make
in upper boughs

or these three nudes
each a hand against
its sturdy trunk?

Vivaldi's *Spring*
echoes across
centuries of rock
and grass

so tentative
its delicate
purchase against
lost time

I carefully
marvelling at the gentle
pastoral scene
a dozen artists
make each

also part of the naked
composition
leaf nor needle nor
blanket
can erase

Sketch 2

Now as a light
breeze wafts
a yellow
shower

of pollen from
the white pine
above
the artists

in a flurry of quick
hands
seek to capture
the beauty

of the models
lovely in their
white

youth
so soft so
delicate

against
the thickening
bark

Sketch 3

Soon they will be gone
even before light
warms breast
and thigh
they will be gone

Even before heat
of summer not yet
upon us not yet
burning the deep
pre-Cambrian rock
they will be gone

Show me. Show me the hand
quicker than
critical eye

Show me the soft flesh
drunk with shadow
escaping light

Siren Song

No rocks in this
composition

but the sky
darkening

over the lake
and a June

breeze
tingling

imminent
rain.

Three nudes
on the veranda

the youngest
leans over

her guitar
and sings

old Baez and
Dylan songs

written before
she was born.

No rocks? Well
not in this

composition
but it may

be youth
and beauty

are danger
enough

no wax in
my ears

to stop
the soft appeal

Fifty Words

If you asked me the essential difference between poetry and prose (though I concede you didn't I'd propose an essay of fifty words or less'd be a pretty sorry thing but take a poem of similar size or thereabouts and chances are it might

It Will Happen Like This

a morning (just
like this one
the spring
sun
glinting through
my glasses one
foot reaching
out to take
the first step
down the stairs
the light
shifting
the weight and solidity
of everything
suddenly gone
vanished
out from under
only this shock
in the heart
falling away
and from somewhere
the pop
of a parachute
opening up
above
like a thoughtful
balloon

Mariposa Elegy (for Greg Curnoe

We make heroes of them
the few who ride
the yellow tenspeeds
of their imagination
invisible
on the black seat
of destiny

who could foretell
that each spoke
tiny in itself
would imply a glass
pane about
to be shattered
on the spinning

wheel become
motionless as
radio news paints
bright circles of
colour on the
beautiful back
road to death